USBORNE FIRST
Level Three

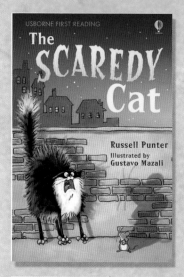

USBORNE FIRST READING

The SCAREDY Cat

Russell Punter
Illustrated by
Gustavo Mazali

USBORNE FIRST READING

The Mouse's Wedding

Retold by Mairi Mackinnon
Illustrated by Frank Endersby

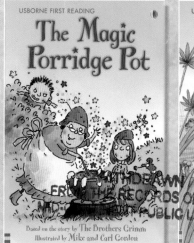

USBORNE FIRST READING

The Magic Porridge Pot

Based on the story by The Brothers Grimm
Illustrated by Mike and Carl Gordon

USBORNE FIRST READING

frogs

Sarah Courtauld
Illustrated by
Jacqueline East

Monkeys

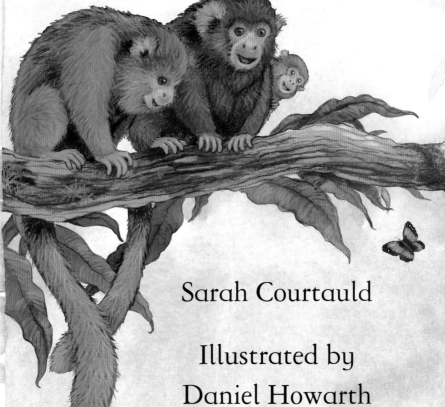

Sarah Courtauld

Illustrated by
Daniel Howarth

Reading Consultant: Alison Kelly
Roehampton University

Monkeys leap
through the jungle.

3

They jump from
tree to tree.

Wheeeeee!

This monkey swings by his long tail.

He grabs a mango to eat.

7

There are lots of different kinds of monkeys. Monkeys with golden fur...

or red faces...

...or long noses

...or big, fluffy ears.

Some monkeys have
bright blue faces

and
bright blue
bottoms too.

Monkeys come in lots of different sizes and they live all over the world.

Pygmy marmoset
Central and South America

Black headed spider monkey
Central America

Cotton top tamarin
South America

Owl monkey
South America

Macaque*
Africa and
Asia

Howler monkey
Central and South America

Baboon
Africa

Mandrill
Africa

* Say mack-ack

You can find
macaque monkeys on
cold, snowy mountains.

They sit in hot water
to keep warm.

Allen monkeys live by muddy rivers.

Diana monkeys live in
hot, wet jungles.

Monkeys are noisy.
When spider monkeys
are excited, they cry out.

Eeek! Eeek!

Eeek! Eeek!

Eeek! Eeek!

19

When these mangabey monkeys see danger coming, they shout.

Whoop! Whoop!

Hooo, ha, hoo, ha!

These happy monkeys sing together.

Wheeee whaaa!

And when the moon comes out, these owl monkeys howl.

AwwWooooo!

Monkeys make faces to
tell each other
how they feel.

These monkeys
are scared.

This monkey is happy.

And this monkey is
very angry indeed.

Baby monkeys stay close to their mothers.

Baby baboons ride on
their mothers' backs.

This mother wants to
jump to the next tree.

But her baby can't
jump that far.

So the mother reaches
out and grabs a branch.

Her baby crawls
across her.

Baby monkeys drink milk from their mothers.

Grown-up monkeys drink water from streams.

They run along branches

to reach tasty fruits.

Monkeys spend hours
cleaning each other.

They pull teeny
tiny bugs out of
their fur

Crunch! Crunch! Crunch!

...and eat them up.

37

Then, the grown-up
monkeys go to sleep in
the sun.

But little monkeys
don't sleep.

They make as
much noise as
they can.

Kek!
Kek!
Kek!

They tickle each
other and run
around fast.

They make silly faces.

They hang
upside down.

They have pretend fights.

Then they make up
with their friends.

They play all day,
until it gets dark.

Then they
cuddle up on
branches...

and sleep until morning.

45

Monkey facts

 The smallest monkey is the pygmy marmoset. It can be just 35cm (14 inches) high, and weighs as much as an apple.

 Some colobus monkeys burp to show they are happy.

 The fastest monkey of all is the patas monkey. It can run at up to 50 km (31 miles) per hour.

 The howler monkey is the loudest monkey. Its call can be heard from 5 km (3 miles) away.

Index

Monkey websites

You can find out more about monkeys by going to the Usborne Quicklinks Website www.usborne-quicklinks.com and typing in the keywords "first reading monkeys". Then click on the link for the website you want to visit.

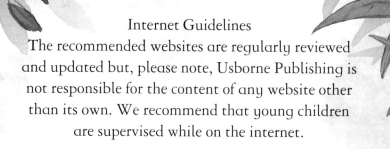

Internet Guidelines
The recommended websites are regularly reviewed
and updated but, please note, Usborne Publishing is
not responsible for the content of any website other
than its own. We recommend that young children
are supervised while on the internet.

Consultant: Marina Kenyon at Monkey World
Designed by Louise Flutter
Series editor: Lesley Sims
Series designer: Russell Punter

First published in 2009 by Usborne Publishing Ltd.,
Usborne House, 83-85 Saffron Hill, London EC1N 8RT, England.
www.usborne.com Copyright © 2009 Usborne Publishing Ltd.

USBORNE FIRST READING
Level Four

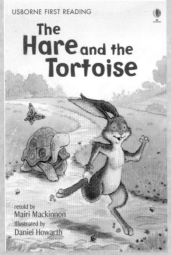